YOU ARE THE BEST!

REAL LOVE

I
LOVE
YOU

XOXO

CUTIE PIE

CUP CAKE

FEBRUARY

SWEET PEA

YOU AND ME

I LOVE YOU

HUG ME

ALL MINE

BE TRUE

SUN SHINE!

ONE I LOVE

YOU'RE SWEET

Thank you for your recent purchase! We hope you've enjoyed your Valentine Coloring Card.
Happy Valentine's Day!
From florabella publishing

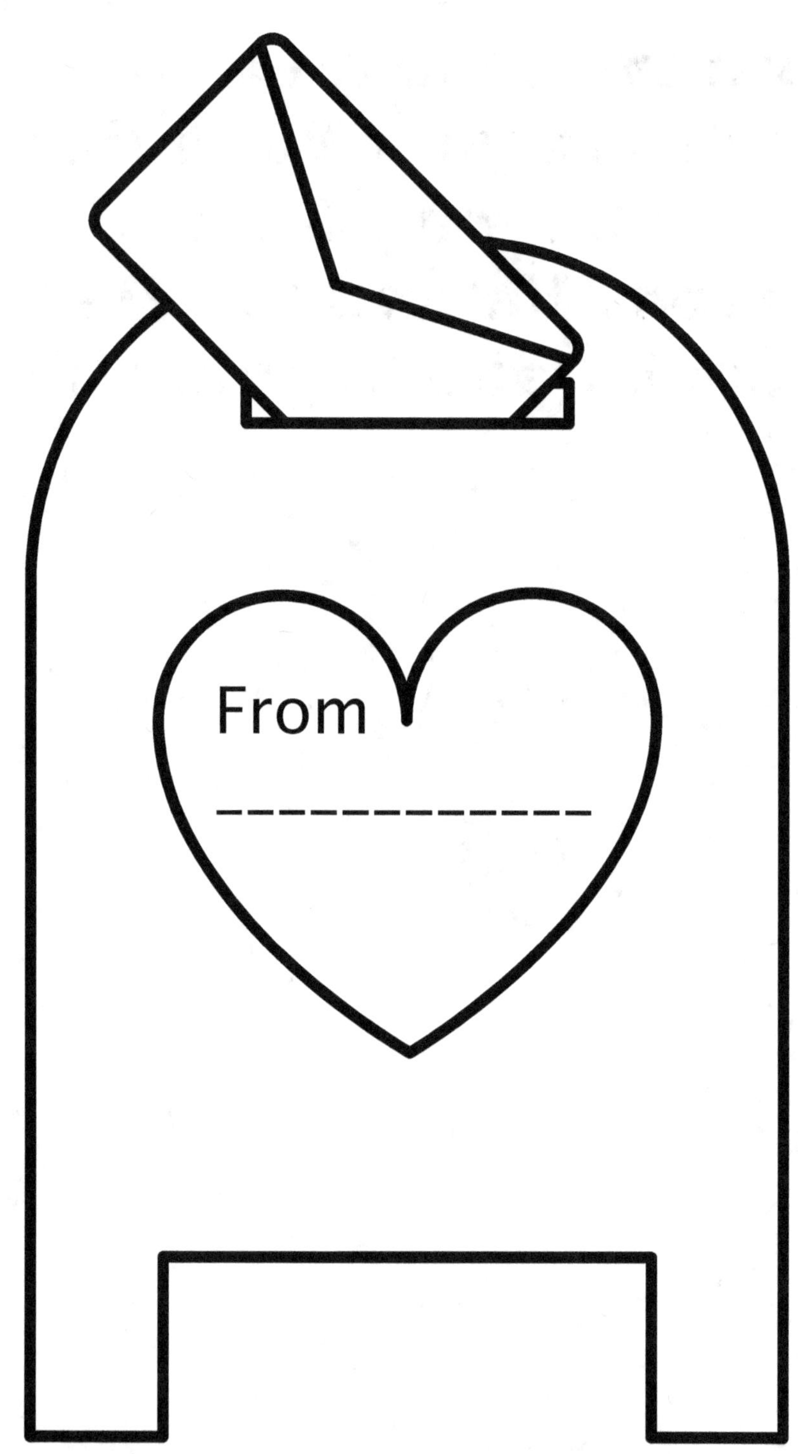

From